Make Us All Islands

Richard Georges

*Make Us
All Islands*

Shearsman Books

First published in the United Kingdom in 2017 by
Shearsman Books
50 Westons Hill Drive
Emersons Green
BRISTOL
BS16 7DF

Shearsman Books Ltd Registered Office
30–31 St. James Place, Mangotsfield, Bristol BS16 9JB
(this address not for correspondence)

www.shearsman.com

ISBN 978-1-84861-527-4

ACKNOWLEDGEMENTS
Thanks for my wife and children, who keep my toes in the earth.

Thanks for the community of writers and readers at Bocas, CaribLit, and *Moko*.

Thanks for Shivanee, Vlad, Lasana, Traci, Andre, Loretta, Jane,
Rajiv, and Sowande who feed me poems in our friendships.

Gratitude to the editors of *Barrelhouse, The Caribbean Writer, Prelude,
The Puritan, Smartish Pace, St. Somewhere, Susumba, sx salon, Under the Radar,
Wasafiri, Where I See the Sun,* and *Interviewing the Caribbean*
where several of these poems first found light.

Contents

Make Us All Islands

Restauradora
sinks in shallow water
Anegada

the clear and calm sea   numerous
sharks and barracuta   diving in the hold
to tear their share from the bodies
                    Robert Schomburgk
                    German naturalist

9

Griot

The African Abednego, tight curls rusting
on his head, cleared his throat and spoke as griots speak.
Gravel shook in his voice like palm fronds rustling.

Every story needs a teller to kindle it,
to keep it burning through light and dark, smouldering
and anointing our heads with the flame's bitterness.

Stories keep light like a fire in the evening,
burning like coal on the tongue of the priestess,
while black saints draped in sargassum sign the old hymns.

The cross of the griot – to speak for the speechless,
to grip the stem of the bone and coral sceptre,
to be mounted, to sing light into the bleakness.

And so, Abednego the griot, the spectre
speaks: *In slav'ry days, the black man's life count for nothing.*
Black limbs fused to the reef praise the breaking slaver,

her wooden cracking cries lost in sea erupting,
her cargo converted by brackish baptism.
The griot drums the ground with his staff. His rusting

head glistens with the sun's anointing. His wisdom
is in long forgotten praise songs, a blank hymnal,
its verses trapped in the holds of divers prisons.

Offering

Wooden ziggurats rot slowly at the bottom
of the columns of this reef.
>>> The slow march of ribbed
>>> barnacles, black tiles in a glittery mosaic,

>>> the cage's rusted lattice, its forgotten aches
>>> are now home to a nervous cloud of silvern fish.

Here Olokun receives his prayers   from skeletons,
whether three or three hundred years beside the eels,

>>> in the *Restauradora*, water filled their lungs,
>>> the grey sharks tore red flesh from limbs still
>>> chained their tongues mute from mourning sun and shore.

>>> The ships and their keels are rooted,
>>> their masts like trees planted in the dense sand.

Birth

The knotted spine of the wreck spat Moses out.
A Spanish basket of oak plank and iron bolt
had held him. The slave ship *Atrevido* boarded,

captured by sword and rifle sprinkled with seasalt.
The black prophet lay below deck with the others,
his destiny tattooed crudely on his forehead,

some greeted these English as their deliverers,
but Moses did not see compassion as they fed
them thin porridge in the boxes they kept them in.

When they gave him to a priest, he knew he was dead.
The old man's heavy cross hung, faith chained
to freedom, slave in all but name.

In the Moment Freedom Comes

The *Atrevido* heaved, rocking itself against
The cobalt breakers. Ungobo could not stand,
sit up, or roll over in her shackles. Again

she felt the ship rock, hang, then fall. She prayed for land
under her breath, others prayed for death in the deep.
Both broke over the din of the relentless waves

No light crept into the boat's hold. There were no days.
In the blackness, the sailors took as they pleased
but they broke in the night with the ship. She awoke

to the chatter of Spanish in the nothingness –
their tongues excited – then a distant cannon fired.
Iron bolts squealed and rough hands pulled each from below.

Naked and shivering in the dark, Ungobo
could trace another boat in the sea's grey distance.

Night fled like a rising mist, her chains, unbroken,
still hung from her wrists. Standing on the wooden deck
sunlight danced deliriously in the shallows.

The kisses of oars to water came next to her.
The men from the rowboats grunted in gutturals
as they plucked them from the hold like fishermen
clearing their traps. She could taste the salt in the air.

The Talking Stone

for Patricia Turnbull

Consider you
*– all who entertain a serious and reverential regard for the resting
place of the departed –*

land measured in quadrants,
    lines on paper –
        distinguishing elevation;

        boundaries –
        where one must and
        must not
                              pass,
        measuring
        how one may –
        and by how much –
                              rise.

Then consider
raising walls stone
by bloody bleached   stone

within which
you build –   family, life,   village.

Then consider
the arc of the hoe and cutlass,
the upturning of hard earth
into dust   only

watered with
salt and blood.
How then
can the calabash   grow?

With what
do we catch our
blessings?

How does
an entire village

disappear?

Redemption

1. THE CHURCH OF THE AFRICANS

The view of the channel from here – the rippling
waters, the rocks that rise from them, and the boats
that sit still as flowers in all this blue loam,
sit still as air cut by hazy morning light
glimmering through yawning louvers
or as songbirds squatting on electric wires.
It is striking seeing the ruined church,
how the roofless rafters seem like a ship's hull.
A wooden hood, capsized and lifeless, set still
on glass. A skeleton of brick and sand remains,
a spectre in daylight. If I could find
in the unroofed cavern the praying shadows
prone and ordered solemnly in pedantic
pews, I would see the rootless vines in salted
shallows, bruised coral wrists reaching upwards.
These folk were survivors. Dream them gripping
snarling rocks as black sea claimed the broken hulk
of their prison. Amidst angry sea-spray coral
heads rise in watery light, their minds routeless,
home as far as Babylon, their salvation
tied to a musket's gaping maw. Nearby,
at the shore, the clear waters babble on.

The Heavy Anchor

The sea   breaks over   the swirling   curls on my
grandfather's head.

His milky teeth   gnaw at the shore,   his mouth sucks
the perforated coral   for salt, water,   and air.

Where else   but the indigo blue   womb of the deep?
Where the records   of these dusty rocks   write themselves
in shifting sands.

Oars knife   the water like spades,
this desert of waves   that grows nothing   but graves.

With what   can we plumb these depths?

What else   but this   blasted   diving
digging gripping   anchor

holding   history   between   its jaws?

ii.

Herons needle the shoreline with their stalking feet
history lies beneath   rotting into nothing.
Each rhythmic wave a cold gesture of erasure
of the trauma of memory   like lashes falling.

Rain falls   like a hail of arrows over our heads.
The conquerors   too   must have mistook the torrents
for poisoned bolts shot   from the green blur overhead
when the first drops rattled against their   iron   morions.

A man must have thought it ignoble to die here
ankle deep   in the mud   and muck of the forest,
hot mocking air sticking   to his neck   his wounds bare
and bloodily formed   by the blade's   crude edges.

iii.

The briny perfume of the sea stirs a reminiscence
of the old hymns that singe our lips

of barks of bastards cleaving the ether,
and the sea's undying roar

of mariner and cargo braving the
unstoppered sky in the corpses of sylvan gods.

iv.

For those moments
in the night
when the rustling
makes you

wonder
if it is
breeze or
rain or
souls

being folded over each other

their tears & spit
sprinkling baptism
on lying flesh.

For rum
lingering on lips
& the embers
of words
smoldering on tongues
the flame caught
in your throat
like a bone
or cough.

For the stickiness
of the night
air & the
heaviness of
the pregnant sky.

For the conch
echoing over
broken shores.

For backs that never
 fully straighten &
the stick that lies
on the steaming ground.

For
Attibon
old-
man broken.

Your tools
are rusted
iron.

Who is left
to show us the way

to our
golden
Tzion?

v.

Baptist George, survivor of the Fancy Me

A graveyard of bone
white coral headstones
line the stony beach of Saona

We went in there Saona that afternoon, an we put the anchor down

and in Road Harbour,

Like this time so, we put down ... put down the anchor down

the sails billow with Saharan winds,
full of the withering sigh of history
the rotting husks of shadowy hulks
mark their place on the horizon,

The more the night come on, the hotter the storm come

never dipping below
the watery lines of
our memory.

And the later it come, the more the storm start to rage

The shovel plunges
as the anchor does
as the seas turn over in rows
and wooden gods rise

start to rage ... start to rage

rise

I see them coming to me, I hear them calling me

their hair foaming
in concentric circles

nobody get where I is ... just myself alone and God

their creaking fingers
writing in the
wet sand.

The Fishermen Measures Life

Azureous fish dart amidst the gold sargassum
while pelicans crouch like gargoyles above, plotting
their winged ambush. The fisherman's visage bares gums

in a grimace contorted at the blaring sun
as he loosens the thick cord from the mangrove's root,
sits, and considers his vessel for a moment.

The citrine paint had faded, the wood underfoot
bruised and splintering, the hull slick with silt and muck.
The fisherman, like his fish, never plots the route

and so, hands black with oil and work grip the tiller,
the outboard snarls and a pelican shifts his weight.
An urchin's ivory carapace seems to glimmer,

and catches his eye amidst the seaweed's shimmer
and the shore's muddiness. The sea gives and she takes
in equal measures – like the slow moan of the reef's

jagged jaws tearing the hull of *Donna Paula*,
her heavy planks splintering into private griefs,
black and white hands gripping at air then sea water.

This patch of sun-seasoned blue opens up to him,
the outrigger's nose lifts gently out the water
which erupts behind 'round the diving pelican.

The yellow hull skips along at a sluggish pace,
the fisherman joined by a dagger-beaked seabird
chasing invisible fish in the creamy wake.

"It is much the same on land," the fisherman thought.
Shark suited men sweat and chase American cash
like fishhooks, mouths transpierced with incandescent lures.

The moment the first tug comes at the jaw,
the shudder of the line first taut, then slack again
as they are pulled aboard dumb-eyed with gasping maw.

The first battered buoy appears aglitter with sun,
its rope, entangled with weed and whelk, peels the pot
from the bed, and as its wooden frame comes to view
the cloudy depths dissolve in slippery shadows.

Proverb

i. Death's ladder is there for all to climb

God
fashion man
from mud
and put him
right back
when he
done.

ii. the one who asks questions doesn't lose his way

a   meandering man   marooned
on this cracked pebble, an ancient wreck –

a   bone in the Atlantic's   throat.

a   wandering woman   waits
on the congress of thrashers in the guava tree –

a   chattering sign-   post.

iii. dead man can't carry dead up de hill

Beneath a cracking sky,

           a jumbie stands on her grave
pointing at the white-washed stones of the cemetery wall.

Here she must draw up

        a femur,
        some philanges, a hip,
        and half a jaw-bone
        to wield at the laughing night.

Her empty eyes measure the hill

    – its steepness, the blindness of its climbing corners –

and the sheer impracticality of her burdens

           laid down at its summit,

her shadowy sockets

        filled with
        the morning's
        bleeding
        light.

iv. rock stone down river bottom don't know when de sun hot

Under the creased concrete bridge,
the ghut trickles a tear. On the slick bank, a rotting rooster rests

wings spread in mocked flight, beak agape in *co*

                                         co

                                                 rico

his silent crows echo a perishing dawn *co*

                                   co

                                         rico.

The water runs cool as a penny under the pillow.

The stone smoothed by flood and famine if asked
could tell of slave and tsunami, or of when it was
a rough rock perched on the hillside

and a radiant rooster crowed *co*

                             co

                                    lo.

v. nicknames are used in case the Devil comes asking

Restricted to notarized documents and letters formed cautiously
in black ink, penned by the dictates and spaces of church and state,
steeple and flag,

        the Devil knocks on doors with a flick of his tail,
and hisses a name between his forked tongue and perfect teeth.

Light Sound Land

The wind on the sea is deafening
voices spat in gales lose their way
and   scatter

The light on the sea is bending
rays shone splinter and we lose
our   sight

The land rises like shaved heads
bowing and shrinking from the
sea's perpetual din.

Landing

A coconut colonnade stands
on the shore watching bodies
disembark,

their hair knotted and uneven,
their limbs too – they walked
like trees do in the wind.

Kingston

If eyes were thrown
over the hill to a village
so named King's Town,
they may expect
to be lost in a lagoon
of quivered cane,
to kiss Obatala's name
for the blessings of rain
and plenty.

But the ears
hear the weight
of Kingston,
and the air's
heaviness does
not hear the
lightness in a
kingdom of dust.

Corpse I

So
the body lying prone
in the gritty surf

can
not resist the probing
of sea and sea foam

nor
direct the Atlantic
past its openings

to
some other propitious
and dumb instrument.

No
body lies still as stone
for the groping sea.

Eshu

Elder,
walk these roads
in peace

Elder,
stretch yourself out
in your sleep.

Elder,
your children
are lost

Elder,
their eyes glaze
like the night

watery
blackness pierced
with steel stars.

Eshu,
the blood sings
for you.

Prosper's Storm

for the man whose death hanged Arthur Hodge

On a rusted hillside, old hymns are sung
along the skirt of a field hemmed by cedars.
Below, the seething sea, a shimmering plain,
covers the stoic crypt where fish take communion
from coral bodies.

The sky uncorks with the firing wind
and the gray tamarind, rotted, rattles like chimes.
The broken drum of thunder beats beats the air
in time, drowning the voice of water,
bird, and beast.

Bodies still break in the earth,
rooted weeds in the shallow dirt.
Here the whip opens the back like a blooming flower
untying knotted muscle from bone
the flesh blushing and peeling in pink petals.
Seaweed snakes the currents

the same way his life slips
down his legs and pools in red muck.
The rod holds no comfort for desperate joys,
its twisted grain slipping and sticking
in the horse shit.

When they loose Prosper
from the tree, the evening
gathering like moths,
the fever is already boiling
beneath his blistered skin.

"Before the gale far out to sea
The hapless vessel went."

"Loss of the Schooner *Fancy Me*"
   – Alphaeus Osario Norman

/1833/
Emancipation

Whereas divers Persons are holden
in Slavery within divers of His Majesty's
Colonies   all such Persons   set free
   An Act for the Abolition of Slavery
   throughout the British Colonies;

/1900/
No viable
industry.

No visible
history.

/1926/
The Loss
of the schooner
Fancy Me

I cannot describe to you
the cries   *of the*
poor

41

For those left behind to ponder a hillside

The cane sways like brown girls on an August Monday.
One brown girl with thick inky hair and a pale dress

washed by hand too many times tilts her head north-west
from a flat patch of grass on Windy Hill where she

supposed to be watching her father's goats. But now
the sun finds her daydreaming above the cane field,

her fingers twirling a braid tied by a peach bow
on a flat patch of grass. Dreaming about that boy

with almond eyes gone away to 'The Land.' Go
away skin as inky as her hair and breathing

hot on her neck, their sudoric bodies heaving.
Is months now cane season start and not one letter

come from San Pedro with "Betty" write across it.
The Atlantic seethes as it batters the island's

shore again, as if it would sever its anchor
and sail east apologetically across it.

Cutter Song

Is only Spanish we does go
our men rise up out their beds
& cut themselves loose of the islands
when they feel the line tug.

Cutlasses were light in their palms
the cane fall easy like the sun
& sweat, sweat that stain
shirts & sheets & breasts.

It have a coconut man from Kingstown
by the market & you could tell
him you want one & he will pull
it from the ice & make it hop
in his hand while the black blade
refuses to shine in two o'clock sun.

The machete is shadow
& it bite the coconut just so.

The machete is shadow
& it bite she neck just so.

A man must live true
like islands surrounded by
a desert of blue.

We dream in poems
& we wake with
ohs that melt in echoes
like photographs
bleached in the sun.

The Fisherman Finds Way

History is as meaningless as heaps of rubble,
or these mossy corpses, prostrate, eager in prayer
and God, the poor carpenter, lonely fisherman

in sweaty toil casting lines that catch only air,
The fisherman stands in his boat
and sees his wake eaten by the sea.

His brown face creases, smoothes, then creases again in
the bright heat. There is no spinning compass, no clear
route home but memory – of rocks, of sand, of gulls

bawling on the beach he measures his life out on
in pounds of iron-eyed grouper, doctor, ol' wife,
for the bright red guts he tosses under the palms

for the starving strays to battle the birds over.
Grains of salt cling to the hair of the copper arm
clutching the black tiller of the outboard motor.

In the reef's dark depths, hulls pass overhead like clouds,
black and ominous, below and above – abyss,
the constant waves rush to meet every crashing bow

and still the fisherman stands pulling in his fish-
pots in burning salt air, pelting rain, until now
turning his boat like a needle pointing the way.

Cane Harvest, La Romana 1918

I.
the cutter wipes the day's sweat from his forehead
his blade wet & ready for the harvest

as the cocolos set this green Gomorrah ablaze
the sparks like fiery prayers sent skywards.

II.
the sun bites at black backs
cutlasses strike the charred cane in concert

each

a blackened god falling in silence.

Rastaman mix earth & blood

                      & seeds with his hands
make something push through the dark soil, make something new.

His graying locks hang in the heat,
                      he thinks of lands
his father worked in La Romana, taut sinews

rising in the day's heat,
                      cutlass in his right hand
the ground beneath soaking in sweat. Blood forms like dew.

On this same hill,
                      where cane used to stand
where his mama used to tend his grandfather's goats,

tilt her head north-west,
                      to feel the rough winds approach,
to listen, to taste it, to imagine a man

far away in a cane field,
                      cutlass in his right hand
nothing else left, facing the angry salted coast.

The sun hangs over the rasta's head like a slave,
beneath his sweating brow,
                      bones of ancestors
bleach in the bitter dirt,
                      his harvest's protectors,
these little relics

                      blessing the pick's pilgrimage.

Redemption

2. LOS COCOLOS

The night rises from the hill like a lean fog
fading, the black sea slowly being gilded
by the peeling horizon. Outside, on the hill,
a fragmented flock stands, still as a painting,
as if awaiting news from the startling sun
over the withering waves. In the smaller hours,
each sound sounds more important against the noiselessness.
Each echo of the yard fowl and thrushie, the groan
as street water rushes through empty pipes,
each note ringing off the hollow air and spreading
somewhere over the sea. The blue desert
of heaving dunes stretches in the graying void.
The cocolo's tongue is mulish, betraying him
around the edges of his words, always sending
him back to that ship a refugee – an exile.
He remembered birds escorting the slow boat
into the brown harbour, great brown seabirds
flying in silence, silver beaked, white chested.
He remembered nothing from before.

The Cutters

The two hired men bend in the heat
fired bronze backs strain, spin,
stretch, their cutlasses swing,
until grass, branches, leaves leap up
over their heads amidst the frangipani
and balisier, flamboyant, oleander.

The old woman stands in the tamarind's shade
Bermuda grass bristling her bare feet.
Her head tied like her hands
her mouth snarls in command,
madras wrapped, dough under her fingernails
her spattered apron clinging to her stomach.

Bushing the Pit

after Winston Molyneaux, coalpit master

First you gather up your guinep, your tamarind, get used
to hearing your axe bawling its songs against their barks.
A man whose job it is to dig the pit takes his grubbing
hoe & makes a depression.

He must know his tool.

Then the man whose job it is to line the runners
descends into the dirt pit to fix them perfectly parallel,
before the wood is stacked for the slow-burning fire
to breathe as we do.

He builds a mound in the ground.

Then the man whose job it is to bush the pit
with coconut palms must know how much to use
for too much will smother the flame, too little will
let the cassie burn to ash.

He cannot afford imperfection.

The man whose job it is to dig the pit
watches the igniting timber

& sees the coal

blushing
in black pots
balanced on blocks.

Wind

In the violet hours, under the palm arcade,
a colony of crows sit with fiery lidless eyes

watching the ethereal sea tumble on,
and the scarred mountains seem to rise,

the trees shudder in a rushing rattle,
a wind moving amongst the bones.

Corpse II

The sloping cedar stoa
guards a bird in Icarian rot,
its grubby feathers spread
like the folds of a mother's frock.

Blue Runner

we must learn again
those arts we have forgotten:

how to throw our hands
up in the shape of a candelabra;

the art of paring
a fish from its translucent bones;

how to pull the thin
shimmering spears from our throats.

Echoes

The haze
stretches like some
yawning thing
against the russet sky

smouldering
above the blue

above
the descending rows
of galvanize roofs
the triangular masts
of swaying yachts.

The blackbird
beats the air like a drum
and the island echoes

with
the knowledge that
*when hunger gets
inside you
nothing*

else

can.

Swing

Under the tamarind tree
grey vines hang like nooses,
swaying in the gentle winds
dying and pendular.

The hurt
sits like a burl
in the throat
knotted
spoiled
dense
groping

gorgeous

when given
the right
varnish.

Tidings

for the 942 who died in the 1853 cholera outbreak

Death come as clear
as a glass of water,
brimming the rim,
wetting the lips with life.

The body swallows
the tide with the rhythm
the shore does
over the sand of the tongue
and its coral mouth.

Pathways run clear
into some place deep
where a secret garden
blooms in the belly.

A Type of Draining

It is a type of draining
we all feel, of a life
desperate to drink
the air outside of
us.

        Water parts the flesh
the way it will mountains,
a river pressing for release
ceaselessly coursing its way
back to the sea.

Kussmaul

Death come still as water
clear as glass in the eye

The body exhales its drying prayers
in a heaving sigh.

The souls are buried
as shallow as the night soil

bowels holding only water as
tender as their faith.

The brittle bodies
wrinkle like pharaohs

their eyes and limbs
blue as the waters that birthed them.

A Place in the Earth

The dumb bodies
lie like leaves
in the dirt.

Death drags
the drying lips back
drawing mouths
into snarls

bracing the teeth
against the whistling
flute of the throat.

The living
philosophise
over the bones

while the yellow love
laughs from the trees
above.

"Then came the men with eyes heavy as anchors
who sank without tombs"

"The Sea is History"
          –Derek Walcott

At the Waterside

i.

In the nascent hours of August, the ferry
lurches towards the grey dock through blue-green waters,
adorned with gold sargassum and white-capped tourists.
Black smoke traces the horizon with a finger
while the old boat's engines cough and spit between waves.
The dockers' shouts crack in the ear like buckshot.
The open sky is cyan, without a wisp of white
and yet wet pebbles drizzle the square I sit in.
I think of another ark pulling down its sails,
a crowd of Tortolans eager to see their sons,
and La Diosa del mar, our Lady of the Sea
brothers chained once more in her coral embrace.
This is a rock with no time for her history,
constructing concrete totems where her cedars groan,
leaving nothing for the bananaquits.
Crowded marinas spread where the mangroves drown
filled with reddened wayfarers on catamarans.
Not even the hands on the captain's wheel are brown
when the sea can segregate, make us all islands.
Then the ochre days when the boat pulls into port
I will remember a schooner sailed by brown hands.

ii.

The sea is as black as the night, reflecting
nothing but the island's apathy. The pale masts,
like obelisks unsure of their foundations,
quiver with the tide. A gannet adjusts his wing.
Behind them, blurred lights flicker across the channel.
It is here where the Empire unravels, crumbling
in Ozymandian ruin – preserving only
an ancient anger held by hands burnt black in sun.
The sea grows darker in intention as it laps
at the rough edges of the shore and licks its teeth.
It is here they find me, a smudge on their blue maps.
The mad ocean stretches thoughtlessly before me,
grinding the shore until white foam sits on the water
like ants who have lost their trail and found misery.
The crests of the waves stampede forward and the
hollow growl of the plane over my head begins
to echo off the islands' cliffs like cannonade.
A white gull tucks his head in his breast and answers.
The fisherman's vessel sits still in the reef
at Buck Island. Something greater covers him
at his rest below these rust and green hills
while sparkling blues betray the reef's lying rocks.

iii.

In the dark morning,
a lone white gull untucks his
beak from his breast and calls
mournfully from the cliffs.

The fisherman sits
still in his dugout

something greater
covers him
at his rest

below these
rusted hills.

Great bending sails
cut the blue horizon

splitting the sky
into uneven portions.

Blooming clouds
hang like the

ghosts of slaves.

iv.

The surf choruses salted ritual,
the crescendo of milky waves churn
the shore rolls up and out
below a deserted sky,
a frigate bird is pinned to the canopy.

Shaded by the seagrapes,
the island takes hold
with grains of sand.

Cedars bloom,
blushing pink through
emerald hills
west to the jagged
granite cliffs
and east
amongst
smatterings
of corrugated roofs.

The seagrape tree
arches over this patch
of sand protectively,
waxen leaves spreading
open to a
single
white
sailed yacht

nodding its way
across the horizon.

v.

I hear the refrain of these snarled trunks
knee deep in sand and memory.
My footprints mimic those of broad backed men,
the whipping waters and the litany of keloids
and the seeping sores of the lash's persuasion.
The salt in the air carries to the plantation
but it is not the same to stand here,
my feet planted surely and washed by frothy wake.
My dog announces, along the beach somewhere,
a discovery – a piece of driftwood not unlike a snake.
I uproot myself, and count my sinking steps
towards his celebrations, the salted voices
singing behind me.

Sea Bath

It is like the matted moss that creeps
on the slatish rock, half buried in dense sand,
licked by the lapping sea.

You wash our daughter in the waters,
wise of the ways the sea can be cleansing,
how the wild brine clears the night's rattling
cough, rinses her nose of thick liquids.

Her protests dissolve in the clear waves,
she glows in the spinning sun.

I wash myself in view of the rippling hills,
baptize myself in this ocean's quiet corners.
A school of translucent minnows appear
beside my legs, feeding on my murky sins.

Waterloo, Trinidad

(for Siewdass Sadhu)

The water is not cold at dusk,
the day withers away
in purples and oranges,
this man's feet like mangroves
in the shallows.

What follows
is not the frigid deep
that mocked his fear.

This salted air
tastes sweet in his nostrils
seasoned with burning cane.

He was not afraid
when the estate men came.

He was not afraid
of laughing men with hammers.

Not when he had seen God
face in black waters
his matted hair in cords
and his power moving
beneath purpling waves.

That was God.
This is Sadhu now
carrying his faith
rock by rock
out into the water.

Ground

There will always be the sea,
beating against this
ground I stand on,
that holds us up in life and
swallows us up,
grinding flesh and bone
to nothing.

A coral chorus blisters the coast
in the gloaming
but this ground
I stand on is
still against
the rigid order of days

still against
the roaring spit of hurricanes
spinning off
the many mouths
of Africa.

This ground
I stand on is
still against
me.

I break
like the sky
in shards.

The Domino Player

A man with a bird's mouth rises
from his easy chair, back bent
with the weight of his years, feet
purpling, swollen with gout.

Anger can stitch a smile to his lips,
his slit eyes yellow like the books
strewn in the rubble around his ruined body.

Amber glasses of rum leave his fingers
as easily as dominoes, the last years
of his life echo in the litany of tiles,
an eternity trying to find
his way back to the sea.

Boiling Bush

The waters train you to remember
what blade of bush can cut
a fever to beads overnight

what broad tongue
can lull your little one
to dream

to swim through the thick night
like darting barracuda.

The waters train you to trust
the steeping leaves
the greenness murkily
flooding the boiling pot

a memory returning
filling the water's
veined spaces.

When the morning
leaves us to ponder
the silt at the bottom of our cups,
the dregs are a remembrance
that cannot be drained.

Leslie

Between the beer bottles and half-filled tumblers of rum or whiskey;
Before I could appreciate these dark and sunny weekday afternoons,
He had me seeing things: German soldiers with funny shaped helmets;
Winston Churchill escaping during The Boer Wars; cowboys.
After a game of cricket and enough trees had been climbed
I bounded home as Hanuman with dusty knees and vision.
A julie-mango if I was lucky – if late, lentil soup or worse.
Even after he had stopped, his gums and lungs were black from exhale.
I forgot how his voice moved in the air, I would forget altogether
When they pulled each tooth out and I sat with him and his pillow.
What little he had to say was muted by the needles then.
On the night he died, we turned the television off.

Passion

The seeds look like eyes   glossy orbs peering
from the fruit's pulp
the hands that roll   what remains
against the sieve

a labour of longing   must sacrifice
persistent knuckle and wrist
for yellow tartness
tempered with the heavy   history of sugar
and work

the speckled fruits   whose carcasses
lie halved, gutted
and spent   sweetness
wrenched through the violence
of hands.

The spider resting on the rafter

                                                     twitches
when my wife switches on the light.

Its legs spread geometrically,
                                          its eyes splice
                            the light into a
                   knitted tapestry of figures

                                                     Toussaint
                                                     Tacky
                                                     ?

It rests there
                        plotting to rob us
                                                of our

common sense with the gourd of its gut

to tie us to sticks, to strike us

                   dumb

                                          with each prickly

limb, to add our story
to those that already
bear his name.

Beating a stone

for Kamau Brathwaite turning 85

On a still day, the blurry clouds sailing slowly
across the lagoon's glass confuses (up from down
sea and sky) until a skipping stone ripples,
distorts, and pauses for islands to bud
blossom like lilies in the places it has struck.

Watch the too black sea beat a rhythm
like calypso on the rocks. These gray and
coppery boulders line the shore,
a chiseled infantry to watch the spray whip up,
its milky froth falling on the level roads
that hem the island

This same too black sea was beating
this same rhythm, frenzied drumming on stones,
the machete falling on too black flesh,
a razored lash keeping the beat.

In the Terminal

The old West Indian men guffawing at the bar
wear their decades in wrinkles on their faces.
Their laughter hangs lewdly in the air,
a rich vibrato falling in the quietest places
of the terminal where it stirs a glare,
a sucking of teeth – here or there.

My nib pushes their lives into the nouns
between my page's pedantic rows.
I regain my pondering of *Tiepolo's Hound*
unfolding my brow's less ordered rolls
measuring my time in hideous cups of coffee,
the pages tick past the hours.
In that moment, the muddy froth hardens
and stains the white ceramic.

Mural

In a feature-
less, dockside dive
I am floating
in the dark waters
of my thoughts

when a man drags
me out dry
by his cough
no
a clearing
of phlegm
in his throat

when my eyes
lock his, he points
at the simmering sea,
aglitter with sun.

"See 'im?"

my eyes
are cast like lines
by his outstretched arm,

at something ruddy
and brown disturbing
the morning's gentle wake

out there.

Out there,
a turtle is somersaulting
under a few mossy bits of seaweed

making them dance
messily on the surface.

I think
I think this
man should
he must be more
than a cook

more than a custodian
of cracking eggs
and sputtering oil

to see
the sea

a writhing mural
of hope and history
always carrying on.

48 Main Street

Long after all his friends, and all his brothers
had shuffled off into some other airy form,
Uncle Cil still made his way like all the others
who had gone before him, step by aching step.
Each waking breath, his old refrain: thank God for life!
A man of quiet accomplishment, when left
with this old piano, its ivory keys,
the notes that faded like his sight in his ear
in the aching light of the day. A man who
still tipped fedoras to people while his knees
found support in gleaming canes. Only a few
will remember Cil soon. The last gentleman
of Road Town. A mythical man to retire
at fifty, perhaps since two of his brothers -
first Irving, then Reggie – did not get to tire
in old age, the fire of youth smothered,
so he spent years traveling with his dear Elaine
until returning to this modest house,
a simple, noble monument that remains
evermore landmarked in my memory.

On the Loss of Lovers

The old lady died of grief,
a black-laced hat, veil shielding her eyes
from the sun. The day before
we wheeled her nearer his casket.

A black-laced hat, veiled to shield her eyes,
sat on her bed next to her bible.
We wheeled her nearer his casket,
mourners made space in the aisle.

I sat on her bed next to her bible,
listening to her breathe as she slept.
Mourners made space in the aisle
for the family and the ceremony.

I listened for her breath. As she slept,
we told stories, the women made bouquets
for the ceremony and the family.
She always had her brandy with him.

We told stories. The women lay bouquets
in the sun the day before.
There was no more brandy with him.
The old lady died of grief.

All Ways are the Sea

i.

The night gathers about its wings
as schoolgirls flutter
in a flock of pleated skirts,
their craning necks no longer powdered
waiting for some back footed duenne
to part the cane
somewhere near
an old man's voice clatters
against his stick which
he waves at the roaming cattle
the village's boys
gathering stones
their buoyant bones
do not alight here
where the sea is always
and all ways are the sea.

ii.

Imagine a rungless ladder
climbed unthinking
above pasture and road
the noble egret in the cow's egress
below the drooping yellow
love light-footed in the muck
the sea mutely chews the bay
like cud, an eternal colonizing
of space, or rock to sand, coast
gazing at the sinking sun
our sins cohere into clinging shadows
faces turned gently into wind
the flesh is still sin
the body the dominion of work
and the sea lies still
a reflecting pane.

iii.

Our bodies are comprised
entirely of elbows and knees
and hips parts that bend
under heat and heaviness
we must wonder what
decency tastes like in
the mouths of the decent
like the frothy fading fog
in the light distance hazing
the infinitely boring horizon
if in the night we disrobe
our skins under tamarinds
and blaze through the emptiness
like comets over the vast
ness of the bay and the openness
of our scars and hearts.

Ghazal of Guyana

Do you see? The bones of stars are falling,
crashing to the earth like trees, like greyed spears

again I find myself amidst a frieze of bodies
lost in our commune of ritual sweat

a hurricane is spinning Saharan
winds through the constellation of islands

they whisper my name from the muddy rows
of cane, reminding me, *the flesh is sin*

the trees ache in the light, their ashen limbs
a warning to birds: *do not alight here*

this tree which is not a way of breathing
of keeping your head above whipping waves

we praise in spit and surf to our God
but not to this sea which is everything

until I can *not* help but think that I
am again: *a flesh and blood poetry*

my sister can remember how to make
baigan, blistering bulbs on splitting flames

on the Parika bank of the river
a boy sells water out of a rice sack

in my office sits a stoic Ganesh
intricately carved out of fiberglass.

Oceans

I once tried to hold the ocean
in my hands, in a glass

in the past, the sea
would grind the bones

of slaves, of sailors
into sand. Even the sand

can be lessened. Like us
when cold water pushes past

lips, teeth, tongue, throat,
into lungs, and all is filled cold.

The ocean is a universe.
An abyss consuming even light in its depth.

What word? What voice moving
over its dark currents?

In my glass, the ocean is radiant,
is effervescent, a mouth tracing the body.

I want to roll an ocean
into a ball in my hands.

I want to hold it up to my eye,
to search for imperfections I know are not there.

I map Africa. America.
Europe. Asia. Continents like

opposing parentheses enclosing nothing
except the histories of too many people.

A broken book of poems,
stanzas falling like shards.

Oceans slip out of me,
Middle Passage, Kala Pani.

I parted your legs and between them
I discover another ocean.

There is an ocean between us
I cannot cross like my ancestors did

And so we all remain. Divided.
Like the shores of islands.

I held an ocean in my mouth,
its cresting waves tickled my palate,

my tongue oared its waves
but I could go nowhere.

The ocean between us has
swallowed the ground, swallowed the sky,

and all of this is only water.

Notes

'Griot', 'Prosper's Storm'

In John Andrew's *The Hanging of Arthur Hodge*, this quote: *'in slav'ry days, the black man' life count for nothing'* is attributed to an elderly man carrying the monomym Abednego. The book details the trial and hanging of slave owner Arthur Hodge, who had murdered the enslaved man Prosper on his plantation.

'Offering', 'Birth', 'In the Moment Freedom Comes', 'The Talking Stone'

Restauradora, Atrevido, Donna Paula are Spanish and Portuguese slave-ships that either wrecked or were captured in Virgin Islands waters after the transatlantic slave trade. Moses and Ungobo are figures whose stories are preserved in historical documents and in Patricia Turnbull's *Can These Stones Talk?*

'Redemption', 'Kingston'

St. Philip's, or The Church of the Africans, is a church built for the community of liberated Africans who settled in the Kingstown area of Tortola.

'The Heavy Anchor'

On the 26th of July 1926, a schooner carrying 89 Virgin Islanders returning from seasonal work in the Dominican Republic's sugar industry sank in a storm. 59 souls were lost. Baptist George, one of the survivors, recounted his experience in Janet D. Smith's *Such are the Hours to Find Peace*.

Lightning Source UK Ltd.
Milton Keynes UK
UKOW04f2356211117

313124UK00001B/143/P